OONA RIVER POEMS

OONA RIVER POEMS

PETER CHRISTENSEN

thistledown press

Thistledown Press Ltd.
410 2nd Ave. North
Saskatoon, Saskatchewan, S7K 2C3
www.thistledownpress.com

Library and Archives Canada Cataloguing in Publication

Title: Oona River poems / Peter Christensen.
Names: Christensen, Peter, 1951- author.
Identifiers: Canadiana 20190066415 | ISBN 9781771871907 (softcover)
Classification: LCC PS8555.H678 O65 2019 | DDC C811/.54—dc23

Front and back cover photographs by Yvonne Christensen
Cover and book design by Jackie Forrie
Printed and bound in Canada

Thistledown Press gratefully acknowledges the financial support of the Canada Council for the Arts, the Saskatchewan Arts Board, and the Government of Canada for its publishing program.

ACKNOWLEDGEMENTS

Some of these poems appeared in other publications, sometimes in a different form: *River of Memory: The Everlasting Columbia, An Eclectic Anthology, Leaf Press Leaflet, Poetry Magazine, Your Daily Poem* and *Duke City Poems*.

CONTENTS

Unrescued

INTRODUCTION

Writing is an act of understanding. To speak clearly of the matters of the heart and earth is critical.

From time to time I stand in front of my library of poetry and choose something singular to read from the many leaflets, chapbooks, soft and hardcover editions. Sometimes I choose a book and read from start to finish, try to absorb the unknowable, hope that the same excellence I enjoy will appear in my work.

I read a lot of history, in particular of the western Canadian local. I am in awe of adventurers and autobiographers for it true that I discovered no rivers, made no first ascents, made no scientific discovery's that changed the fate of humankind. When I set my poems among the accomplishments of truly great heroes, I am deeply humbled.

That said my endeavor has been to arrange words so they cast light on our human affairs and natural condition. I am truly indebted to Thistledown Press for their support and faith in my writing. Thank you to John Lent my keen-eyed editor. And to the gracious and indomitable Eastend Arts Council for the Wallace Stegner Grant for the Arts which included a month long residence at the Wallace Stegner House in Eastend where *Oona River Poems* was completed. And to Yvonne, editor, partner and love of my life; thank you for your support.

There are many voices that speak through these poems; many poems stand on their own, others provide context to the whole and the solitary life of Peter Christensen, 67, poet, survivor, and witness.

"*The more we persist in misunderstanding the phenomena of life, the more we analyze them out into strange finalities and complex purposes of our own; the more we involve ourselves in sadness, absurdity and despair. But it does not matter much, because no despair of ours can alter the reality of things, or stain the joy of the cosmic dance which is always there. Indeed, we are in the midst of it, and it is in the midst of us, for it beats in our very blood, whether we want it to or not.*"
— Thomas Merton *New Seeds of Contemplation*

"*. . . decency is a gesture of good faith in the ability of others to testify.*"
— Racheal Shields as quoted by William Ramp in *Weekly Hubris* "An Admonition"

"*Cowboyin' is something that you do because you can't not do it.*"

WHEN THE TIDE COMES IN

When the tide comes in
Let the roaring waves
With the love of God
Sweep across your soul
Like a mighty flood
When the tide comes in

— Chorus Salvation Army hymn *When the Tide Comes In* (*found in a hymnal in the Salvation Army church at Kitkatla.*)

A SURPRISING SWEET TASTE

It has been a storm-wracked week
even Billy G
brought *Trooper 1*
into the harbour
for a couple of nights
unusual for him
not to anchor
somewhere near
where he is trawling
for shrimp
this time of year

As we talked
he was heading
his last catch shovelled
a two gallon pail
full of fresh shrimp
gave them to me
said they had a price
I would like

Lutz caught four fat salmon
on Monday
gave us two deep red fillets
said we should invite him and Wendy
over for dinner

I set a smelt net in the harbour
caught a couple dozen
dipped them in flour whole
added salt and pepper
placed them in a hot skillet
full of sizzling olive oil
fried till crisp
a surprising sweet taste

TOP PREDATOR

"In life itself, there is no reconciling, systemizing, no under-standing: we just live it and all is well with us."
— Daisetsu Teitaro Suzuki from *Zen Buddhism*

The tide comes in and
with it Northern Shovelers,
Mallards, Buffleheads,
Harlequins, a Harbour Seal
and Bill — all fishers
of the coast

A top predator
has no doubts
only expenses
sees clearly
what's to be done

No high mass for the deceased
no cocktail sensitivities
nor brow-furrowing conundrums

Apparent contradictions do not worry
the processing of animals into product
on the working deck of *Trooper 1*

He prepares his catch
champagne environmentalists sip
their chardonnays and tattle
enjoy their shrimp parfait

BITTER CANDY

A friend sends a poem
his adulterous wife
has run away
with the dog trainer
some joke he says

Bitter candy
difficult because of its content
hell, the whole poem is nothing *but* content...

Such useless words

He offers an admonition
to the offspring
Cast no stones
be bigger than
what has happened

Time will heal
but not replace
these wounds

Why these trials
I ask

No answer

just the cold blind
comfortless hope
that we will
get through

there are things
yet to be done

2ND AVENUE RUPERT

A four beat
boom boxes out of
the trunk of a Ford Fiesta
recklessly cruising 2nd Avenue

A noisy procession
into the primal

Fuming down the street

Pissing evil

Leaving only the smell
of exhaust

CITY OF RAINBOWS

I am standing in line at Tim Hortons
and by chance at the end
of a rainbow

I think of this town like that:
end of the rainbow
edge of the continent
end of the road

People drive like crazy
up and down Second and Third Avenues
never could figure this out
I mean past First is just ocean
so what's the hurry

I give way to a young girl
with a baby in her arms
her boyfriend stands shuffling behind
his do-nothing hat on sideways
his T-shirt warning:
Mouth operates Faster than Brain

Prince Rupert
city of rainbows
covered in native motif tattoos

on the street
I watch out for traffic
especially the humped-up one-tons
with straight pipes and knobby tires
decals in the back window
young males behind the wheel
I like the place

no suits
just pilgrims and aboriginals
searching
for fish, welfare, basketballs, jobs,
payday loans and money market dreams

CUMSHEWA

God put deer on the earth
for me to eat

if I was Hindu or Buddhist
or postmodern
I might prefer the killing
be done by others
and buy my protein
safely wrapped in plastic
keep my distance
from what is animal

Here on the North Coast
I am "cumshewa"
slang for driftwood or
what some call us "Whiteys"

I do my own killing

shed my own tears

HEARING LOSS

Years ago
I could hear a grasshopper
clicking in the grass

now age is feasting on me
the big machines
working nearby
seem far away
no trucks squeal or rumble
barking engines a dull roar

I rarely hear birds sing
boats come and go silently
leaves do not rustle
and the wind makes no sound

There is a constant ringing
in my left ear
tinnitus they call it
I wear hearing aids now

If the speakers face me
and keep their heads up
I try to read their lips
in order to help interpret
what is being said

Pardon me, sorry, huh, say again?

I try their patience
say it with a laugh

better deaf than dead

better to hear some things
than not hear at all

MANLIFT

The two of you
estranged father and son
sit stiffly on a bench
in front of Home Depot
where I dropped you off
an hour ago

He's between jobs
has taken time to meet with you
on neutral ground

is solid looking
offers his hand
confident in what he has become
neither arrogant nor too proud

I like him

Later I find you both
sprawled against a blue manlift
parked on this hot day
in the shade of Russian Willows
along a cool creek

and that is where
you shake hands with him
give him a big hug

he returns it

We all know
something good happened
but on our way home
are unsure of it
only agreeing that
hope is surely the path
to lost children

FISHERS

As it turned out
brother Hans caught all the fish
the Accountant
caught none
and by day's end
became despondent
finally getting in my face
over his negligence
(my opinion)
in minding the lead balls
attached to the down rigger
two of which detached
and made their way
$44 at a time
down to the seabed
where they joined
millions of dollars' worth of
jigs, spoons, flashers, nets, weights,
hooks, rods, reels, swivels, outboards
and other mistakes festooning the bottom
of Barkley Sound

Accountants (it seems)
are a humourless tribe
when at the end of the day
they are faced with a deficit of fish

they have not the grace of poets
who always catch something

FORESHORE

*"So simple it can be with everything one silently knows about
but finds it pointless to talk about."*
— Harry Martinson from *Wild Banquet: Nature Poems*

Some folks are all worked up
because Bobby
has a cluster
of derelict boats
leaning this way and that
in front of his boatshed

He said
"I'll be gone out of here soon enough."

He could have told them
a few old boats
on the foreshore
are a good buffer
against ruin
or
a derelict-free shore
erodes quickly in a storm
but who would see the sense in that

SHOVELLING SNOW

He was a good man
honest, forthright and competent

worked in the service of his community

I thought
he looked out
through wry eyes
taking in the highway
along which
he made his living
fixing cars

They said
he was shovelling snow
around the garage
early in the morning
and shot himself
by accident

There are questions
one must ask

but what the hell
would we living
know about dying

ONLY TWELVE

Is it possible
that only twelve
full time residents
could have a greater
number of human foibles and problems:
envy, cancer, obesity, vascular disease,
bursitis, broken hearts, hoarding, mental illness, old age,
idiosyncrasies, eccentricities, diabetes, drunkenness,
kidney and Crone's
disease, arrhythmia
and much much more

only twelve of us
and this much trouble spread around

yet not one of us would let the other drown

EVIDENCE

Witness the river that flows
count the waves coming ashore
each carrying possibilities
of drowning in
the cold green water
in which my small earth skiff scuffles

If my life never amounts to much
and some things don't get done
let us just say it was because
it rained too much or
the sun shone or
my thinking was cloudy or
I did not pursue direct objects or
locate myself among real things

So delicious the local when
united with the senses

SOMEWHERE IN THE HEAVENS

As cold and warm air kiss
winds thrust clouds
tangle jagged rocks

somewhere in the heavens
a river begins

water cuts
the crust of the earth
fractures light
tints azure lakes

a river becomes an ocean
a mind settles after turmoil

STORM SURGES

We have moved
as far away from
most people as is practical

Five families live here
separated from the mainland town
by winter storms
in from Hecate Strait

to get here
you must know
when tidal rapids run hard
where kelp beds mark silent rocks
when the tongues of the Skeena River
reach for the unwary

During winter
we study marine forecasts
a week in advance
of travel to identify
"weather windows"
avoid the boat killing storms
muscling in from Kamchatka
and the Gulf of Alaska

Spring tides running with
storm force southern winds
push the sea
up the Grenville
past the harbour
over the river bank
until the lower step
into our house
is flooded

From the thwart of the small skiff
you are rowing
to cross the driveway to the woodshed
you shout
"Is this isolated enough for you?"

I answer, "I am not nearly
so afraid of high tides
as I am that you
will stop loving me."

LOS HERMANOS DE OONA RIVER

It is Easter break
quite a few kids
and young mothers
are out from town

They make a big deal out of Easter
tie dying T-shirts
egg painting
kite flying
campfires
an Easter egg hunt

On the long weekend
the men and their guests
will arrive
there will be a fund-raising auction
at the hall

no Los Hermanos of a flagellant order
abide here
no ritual penitent-like crucifixions
are practised

although after the long winter
small communities
being what they are
sometimes there is cause

MEETING THE BIG BOAT

"It is time for all the heroes to go home
if they have any, time for all us common ones
to locate ourselves by the real things we live by."
— William Stafford, *Allegiances*

Nosing the skiff out
from behind the seawall
into the tea-coloured river
then into the stiffening south-east wind
I point toward the *Tshimshian Storm*
hove-to in deeper waters
waiting to disembark passengers
groceries and gear

Pounding through the tangle
of standing waves menacing the bar
I take shelter in the lee of the ship
throw the deckhand a line

the skiff bangs and scrapes
against the rolling hull of the ship
while bundles and boxes get handed down

two big men slip aboard

and we leave the shelter of the ship
turn our backs to the wind
to surf the swell

Loaded over-loaded
green water slopping over the gunnels
the skiff wallows
humps and teeters
past the dolphins

that mark the fairway
leading to the harbour

Out of the wind
behind the breakwater
we tie tightly to the pier

unload the groceries and boxes
grin and explain to one another
that it was marginal just marginal

we lick beads of water
from our cold etched knuckles
taste salt and the
real things we live by

MIRACLES

My nextdoor neighbour
burns his garbage on the river bank
sends putrid smoke upriver on the south wind

tin cans and plastic bags drift upstream
with the incoming tide
to lie on the river bank
in front of our house

Another neighbor wants me to
write letters to Government
grind some grist
but I claim I am shy
about my gift
with words

I am told
my boat doesn't fit in
and when am I going to get
something more practical
and
that I should not
take certain kinds of work
others might need

You really would not want to
enjoy the day outwardly
for someone is sure to launch
an arrow at such optimism

but there are miracles

my garbageburning neighbour
called to warn me

that the big grey wolf
was in his yard today
and so I should be wary
for the care of my little black dog

thank you I said
thank you

THE LONG TONGUE OF THE RIVER

reaches the ocean
tastes salt
whispers stories
to green estuaries
and holothurians
of rumbling creeks
black bears
cottonwoods
and ponderosa pine

Where do people
in this ecosystem fit
homeless wanderers
tongues full of ideas
of conquering
of organization
of balancing nature

SPRING RAINS

Misty rain, heavy rain,
light rain, driven rain,
wet rain, gentle rain,
drizzle, showers,
downpours,
stormy rain,
sideways rain,
freezing rain,
cold rain,
pouring rain

our little house on the river
sheds the weather

we are warm and dry

FAIRVIEW HARBOUR

Old fishing boats surround us
wood, iron, glass
built to last:
Savage Eagle, Royal Pride,
Nemesis, the big draggers
work nearly done,
one troller left

the *Nicole Rai*
still rigged, her poles held high
and rattling in the building southeast wind

A few gillnetters
tied tight to the dock
Crisis and *Winter Green*
their decks worn but clean
scrubbed down by someone
who still gives a damn

the rest of the penitent fleet
is covered in black and green scum
covered in regret and neglect
bureaucratic bungling
debt and unpaid moorage

CARBONISTAS

While exempting themselves
from oily sins
and living large
behind their academic curtains

the hypermobilized saints
and prophets
of deep ecology
expend themselves
delivering anthropocene sermons
from their mansions
overlooking Vancouver harbour
and Carthage Tennessee

These carbonistas
burn only sanctified kerosene
as they jet around the globe
from podium to podium

Leaning back into their seats
they stretch their legs
enjoy fine wines
polish their speeches
that will counsel
the pensionless hordes
and unsalaried elders
to cut back stay home spend less
in order to replenish
the carbonistas' non-taxable
collection plates
thereby ensuring
salvation through
science

FISHERS

Tongues
full of ecology
and conservation
stand in the river

hooking fish
sluicing them
toying with them
till they are half-dead

their jerking rods
give shape and feel
to the struggle for life

Having dropped some cash
in local stores
where merchants
speak in restless tongues
of rivers alive with the sound
of engines from Japan
the Recreationists disappear
up the asphalt slabs
that delivered them

To live as a fish
is to live without
hatred or jealousy
if you have need
of such a fish friend
take one home and eat it
leave the rest for there is
struggle enough in all our lives

THE RIVER TAKES A LIFE

"When stories are told retell them the way they were told,
they are given to you that way so that you can retell them,
not rewrite them."
— Barry Lopez, *Winter Count*

"I know what happened
I have been there many times myself.
He was standing beside the boat,
started the engine,
then hopped in.
The engine quit,
so he went forward
threw out the anchor
but it didn't hold.
Sometimes it doesn't hold.
The boat drifted into a sweeper
That caused the boat to flip.
The boat swung and the
motor hit him on the head.
There was a big bruise
on his head.
The funeral's later today.

It wasn't just one thing.
Starting the engine
from outside the boat,
losing the anchor,
being too far forward,
the sweeper.
Flipping the boat.
No, it's never just one thing."

MONSTERS

Disorientation descends
as we fog sail
our little ship
into the vague world
of a broadening Grenville Channel

no up or down
or forward motion

only the small wave
our boat arouses
tells us we are moving

Our radar warns us
of a fast intruder
its long loud blast scares us senseless

a minute later we roll till
books empty onto the floor

another fast ship follows
I blindly cut across its wake
split a steep white crest

As the sea settles
there is great relief in our hoary world
and we grasp the wind
that has travelled so far
to feather our cheeks
push the boat forward
split the waves

RECONCILIATION

I feel
no honest pride
in owning this land
for it seems
we were entitled by pirates

and no matter how Queenly
the bureaucrats make our claim
no matter that our forefathers and mothers
were innocent or refugees
it seems we are here
by thievery and conquest
and must reconcile

So where better to start
than on these stolen shores
at the dock
to buy fish from the "Indians"

fish the Feds say is not theirs to sell

We line up do a brisk and fair business
for the cleaned and shiny sockeye

as I hand over the money
he exclaims with a wry smile
"If I had known this place had so much money
I would have robbed it long ago."

I laugh and take my tote full
of fish to the truck
scan the channel for Feds
offer thanks
to the old totems
of the sea and land

COLLABORATIVE MANAGEMENT AGREEMENTS

Show me the Bill of Sale!
Show me the Bill of Sale!
shouts James Bryant
Hereditary Chief of the Tshimshian
as we bureaucrats huddle
over our colonial fixing
convinced that nothing good
can exist outside our heads

Tarted up with epaulets
and green badges
we hide our faces
behind chicken masks
and negotiate from positions
of imagined power
entitlement

We begin the meeting
by reading the preface
in which
we have put a proviso

that says
should we want out
we can dissolve
this (ersatz) agreement
at any time

they stick in a disclaimer
that says
should they want out
they can dissolve
this agreement
at any time

We know
that higher level Bureaucrats
are still intent
on colonizing
will break these promises

They know
other Chiefs will
want more wampum
before they sign

Show Me the Bill of Sale!
says James

Then the greasing begins

we puff up our chests
draw deep breaths
eye each other
get down to business

NO PLACE FOR A MAN IN A SMALL BOAT

The tidal river of Masset Sound
wells up against the south-east wind

deep bow-shaped waves toss spindrift
into white mist

cormorants dive deeply
from shoreline boulders
into marauding currents
running hard
into this inland sea

Looking upon the foment
I am satisfied these cold grey waves
are no place for a man in a small boat
no place for lies or half-truths or
for those without faith
in the existence of god
new age relativity
or after-death dimensions

for once the bulwark is breeched
faith or no
the sound will claim its corpses
choose a trophic path
for drifters

The flood tide
aggrieved by southeast winds
and impassable
turns twice a day
bound to moon and sun
is unforgiving proof
of consequences

This stormy day
I am content
to just stay home

BILLY BAY

At Billy Bay his ghost
walks the dikes
he built to push back the tide
and create a garden

Billy had heard that in Canada poor men could prosper,
escape falling on the sword, the Bushido way of dying.
This remote bay a refuge from the *Whites*;
best to be left alone.

Every day he filled his wheel barrow
with rocks and dirt
and pushed it
to the end of the dikes
to lengthen his earthen barricades
wove cedar branches in for strength
built flood gates
to drain the sea grass meadows
planted potatoes for prosperity
fished for need
and to sell to the canneries
The Feds came to take census
and when Pearl Harbour was bombed
the roundup began

Dispossessed of property and possessions by the Custodian of
Enemy Aliens Billy was

put to work on road gangs
far from the sea
his wife and children
sent to internment camp

After the war
Billy was given a choice

exile to Japan
or move east of the Rockies
where he could
prove his loyalty to Canada
by hoeing sugar beets

Billy Bay
just a name
on a chart
his cabins sacked by
back to the landers and draft dodgers

but today I am walking Billy's dikes
they stand as strong as ever
still contain his dreams

Unrescued

"Before you have studied Zen, mountains are mountains and rivers are rivers; while you are studying it, mountains are no longer mountains and rivers are no longer rivers; but once you have had Enlightenment, mountains are once again mountains and rivers are rivers."
— Daisetsu Teitaro Suzuki, *Zen Buddhism*

"Love is there to help your loneliness, prayer is to end your sense of separation with the source of things."
— Leonard Cohen

"How heavy it all is, all that I suddenly have to carry, how heavy it is for the butterfly to tow the barge."
— Thomas Transtomer, *The Blue House*

ANGLZ HAIR AND TANNING SALON

At *Anglz Hair and Tanning Salon*
I opt for the wash
and lean back into
the curve of the basin

Nicholas massages
then washes my hair
conditions my scalp

I nearly sleep
then am ushered
to the barber's chair
where in the flawless mirror
I am free to gaze
upon my image as much
as it pleases me

Nicholas begins to snip
but I sense he is restless
without talk
so I ask about his homeland

Savouring this bit of fruit
he takes a deep breath
and explains that his people
were globalized farmers
unable to compete in
Europe's Common Market and
so immigrated to Canada

He paints word pictures
of tinted glass jars
filled with slices of
sun-blackened Roma tomatoes
suspended in glinting cold pressed olive oil

a sweltering day at the market
patrons lined up at every stall

As an afterthought
he points out that his cousin
owns land on a mountainside
where water is near and that
one day
when he has styled his last head
he will return and farm again

He pauses

to gauge my head
as if it
might be a ripening tomato
then puckers his lips
as he bites and kisses
a plump succulent fig
the king of fruits he explains

I close my eyes
imagine he and I walking
arm in arm like brothers
through rustling olive groves
singing fruitful anthems
a faded blue salty sea behind us
succulent slices of flawless figs
floating beneath the clouds above us
birds soaring higher and higher on
the prickly heat
of a Mediterranean sun

Suddenly
Nicholas sweeps

turns my chair and
mirrors the back of my head
a perfect haircut

Nicholas and I
walk to the till
are at peace today
with the purposes of immigration
beauty salon esthetics
and November

KAREN

Once I thought beauty
perfect women
languishing in glossy magazines
but later realized
such images
were commissioned
by purveyors of tools
whoremasters and transportation kings
to grease the transubstantiation
of desire
into need and spending

After that I turned away from beauty
but then Karen
my philosophy queen
asked
"Do the mountains exist behind the fog?"
and I had to answer "Yes."
because we have reasoned it is so

For Karen Hersey

BRINGING UP THE PAST

One day a man
was working
the colonial landscape
and picked up an artifact
of unknown origin

He had stepped down
from his tractor
to adjust its machinery
and saw on the freshly
turned soil
a small spear point
he bent to pick it up
examined it and
put in his pocket

As he plowed
the past crop under
he wondered if
the 7/16 openend wrench
he had left lying
on the beam
of the cultivator
would one day be discovered
by a future worker of this land

This thought followed him
for a few rounds of the field
but by the time
he finished plowing
he had forgotten
the spear point

One day a woman
was emptying
her husband's pants pocket
when she cut her hand
on a small spear point

When she showed her husband
he said he had been working
in the landscape
stopped his tractor
to adjust machinery
and had seen it shining
against the black soil
had picked it up and
put it in his pocket

As he continued to make
rounds
he wondered if someday
someone would find
in the field
the 7/16 openend wrench
he had left lying
on the beam of the cultivator

She said,
"Spear points
are dangerous and
you should be more careful
about what you put in your
pants pockets"

While emptying his pants
his wife cut her hand
on the spear point
and said he should be more
careful
before turning his pants in for
washing

He replied that he had kept
the spear point
because it reminded him
that the land had a past
"So does my hand" she said

He said finding the spear point
had reminded him
that the land had a past
"Maybe so." she said
"But the next time
you need the laundry done
you can wash the past
out of your own pants."

The husband thought to himself
sometimes
it was just not worth
bringing up the past

CHEESECAKE

Hard
to believe
she is gone

not among us

a mother of two boys
a health-care professional
a nurse
you just knew
she held family and friends
close

One time
at their house
she was standing by the window
watching her garden grow
eating very little
staying trim I supposed
but I saw her gorge
on a second dessert

I looked at her in mock surprise

She wiped a big piece of cake
from the corner of her mouth
and turned toward us watchers
with a smile that let us know
that she was not as "perfect"
as everyone so nicely insisted she was
and then she laughed
and said as though
she was beauty itself

"More cheesecake everyone.
Please have more cheesecake!"

For Dorothy

CHERRY BLOSSOMS

Ah cherry blossoms
freedom
living someone else's life

Ah cherry blossoms
freedom
living your own life

Ah Cherry blossoms
so little time

GAIA HYPOTHESIS

We were sitting
looking down the river

You said
"I believe in the earth
and the river;
they are spiritual things."

"Don't you think such beliefs
are just something
made up to comfort us
because we are afraid of dying?"

"Yes." you said

CANADA DAY: LAKE WINDERMERE

Hotter than blazes today
in the near empty parking lot
of the President's Choice

I'm waiting for Yvonne
to emerge from the "No Frills"
with chips

Am thinking
everything's secularized these days
shopping, war, theft, even national holidays

What does it matter the day
as long as the store's open

not busy though

tarmac's hot grey molten

A black Cadillac Escalade
in dark glass cruises in
sniffs around
parks
sweat dripping from its
air conditioning unit

He stays with the car
keeps the big engine running
to stay cool
while she
coiffured, spike-heeled
and wearing a diamond

as big as a BC cherry
rumps across the sticky pavement
in an awkward run
to the automatic yellow doors

She returns with twin bags of ice
clutched to her breasts
ice for the offspring I bet
who in frothy Wake-Boats roar
around and around
a small cerulean lake
turning it to mud

EDENIC MOMENTS

Unlike many who made journeys
to put their name on things
so they could rush home
and sell their memories
I was a simple pilgrim,
a kind of holy man
if you will allow,
wandering in the wilderness
seeking edenic moments

When I did return home
I unloaded my saddles with deliberation
set the sweat-heavy blankets out in the sun to dry
made the restless horses stand
tied again to cool down
while I brushed
the sweat and dust
from their backs and legs
the tangles from their tails,
then loosed them to roll
in the thick grey dust of the corral

They would shake it off
in a storm
then stand and stare at me
as if to say they knew darn well
I had just brushed them down
but damnit the dirt
they just packed into their hides
will keep the low elevation flies at bay
until the next trip

BOULDERADO

"If you don't like what you see on the page change yourself."
— Keith Wilson at Las Cruces

It was pre Berlin Wall coming down
rice paddies still smoldering in Viet Nam
après amnesty for draft dodgers
and a little edge left on America
when I heard Ginsberg and Wall
read in a Boulder Colorado church
to protest war

Way too proud
of choosing
not to be
a *good ole boy*
Ginsberg cranked his organ
and sang his poems
in a booze-scarred voice
that bragged on and on
about having the power
not to bomb

This legend was
just too Amerikan

After the reading
we gathered around a table
at the Bouldarado
an upscale watering hole
where a Japanese Walking Poet
elbowed his way in

strutted his stuff
Ginsburg and Wall gave way

It had been a hot summer day
I was wearing a white T- shirt
a broadbrimmed straw Stetson

The Japanese Walking Poet
the New Yorker
and the Slender Complainer
all of whom had gathered
earlier at the Anglican Church
to read poetry protesting war
made it clear
by closing their circle
that Canadian *cowboy* poets were uncool
were rednecks,
dirt, not welcome
at their New York cum Boulderado conclave
I know what it means
when a circle closes you out
I've seen animals do it
to protect themselves

After that I lost interest
in New York howlers
Slender Complainers
and Walking Poets
it seemed to me
their spirits were broken
and like spoiled horses
they had become malicious
or maybe
it was just they were too proudcut

THE BOTANIST RETURNS FROM LHASA

*"Zen in its essence is the art of seeing into the nature of one's
own being, and it points the way from bondage to freedom."*
— Daitaro Teitaro Suzuki *Essays on Zen Buddhism*

In the small grassland pasture
next to her house in Windermere
the neighbour ran too many horses
turned the pasture to dust and weeds

She asked him to cut down the number
but he refused and answered by mounting
two spotlights on his garage
so their beams shone in her windows.

Then
the neighbour hauled in
the skeleton of an old truck
and positioned it on his property
twenty feet from her front door

Then
the neighbour hauled in
truckload after truckload
of horse manure and dumped it
by the fence next to her back door

Then
the neighbour mounted loudspeakers
on the back of his shed
pointed them toward her house
played boom box noise day and night

"This is what neighbours are for"
she said "to practice Zen."

put her house for sale
moved to a place
where no animals graze
where the hills are steep
wet and rugged
where pastures were
long ago covered in asphalt and houses

"You don't know how lucky you are to have seen grasslands in a
pristine state," She said as she told her story.

"In the hills around Lhasa
great great grandfathers
have only seen overgrazed pastures."

FISHING TRIPS

Prayer and love are learned in the hours when prayer has
become impossible and your heart has turned to stone.
— Thomas Merton, *Seeds of Contemplation*

When it came to fishing
you had to keep catching and catching
from early dawn 'till dark
the number
mattering more
than lakes or sky or forest

Just catching and catching those poor damn fish

It was the fishing trip from hell
as it seemed to me
it was disrespectful
to treat fish like toys
I mean to count them like that
fish after fish hooked
dragged in
thrown back
some to die for nothing

There was so much booze and food and cigars
we didn't even eat the fish we kept

Some kind of manliness

Under a night sky so clear and holy
on that northern granite shield
surrounded by ancient Spruce
I harboured high-minded ideas

about fish
couldn't understand why someone
would drive three thousand miles
to treat food that way

After that we dropped away
from each other
you becoming lost in the past
building a museum
last I heard

Me, drifting
from job to job
picking up a few
readings now and then
my poems turned to dust
in my mouth

Looking back
nothing makes sense
not my assumptions
or my values
or being so hurt
about people using up fish
for nothing

I had settled into the kind of anger
I was afraid of when I was young
the kind I had seen good people harden into
and not be able to quit

Now that time has eaten us
here we are
agreeing

that we have been
in each other's lives
all these years

the common thread
— fear of dying —
has luckily brought
us together again

UNEMPLOYED

The machine hovers offslope

we rush to fall two big trees
the new pilot says
are too close
to the landing platform
we have cribbed
to the side of the mountain
so the machine
can toe in

The tree my friend is falling
swings ninety degrees downslope
whacks me to the ground.

Pinned in a hollow
knocked unconscious
tree across the gap
my legs below

I revive to voices calling me back
to the whopping thrash of the machine
parked above us

stunned but moving
I crawl up through the framework
of the platform
and into the chopper
bent but not broken

Meanwhile
last night's rain
washes heat

from the cerulean blue dome

a wisp of cloud

not a lot going on
guess
he doesn't want me around
anymore
reminding him or others
that he fucked up

UNRESCUED

1.

West of Calgary a yearling black bear was struck by a vehicle. It was a well-known animal because it foraged on grain in a field near the highway.

An autopsy was performed

Inside the bear's belly
was found:
a handful of activists
a pack of bureaucrats
a minority of wildlife biologists
and a faction of the general public

Before the autopsy released them from the bear's belly this group held an emergency meeting where they formed a consensus. This is what they agreed upon:

it would have been good for
this bear to wake up next spring
in its home range
as a wild free bear
healed as best it could
from an injury
the bear should never have suffered.

2.

After further investigation it came to light that some of the people living in the bear's belly had wanted the bear captured and taken to a rehab facility; they were angry that the Fish & Wildlife people had decided to leave the bear unrescued. A prominent activist who had been living in the bear's belly for a long time commented that:

living free in the wild
is not something any bear
should have to give up
just because *we* think
it would do better in captive care

he argued that wounded bears would heal just as fast if left to
forage in the wild. His biggest concern about bears like this one
was that the bear would be kept distracted and alert by people

viewing it when it should be
left in peace
to fatten up
so that
it could complete
the healing process
in its den during winter

he said we have a human impulse to try and intervene in situa-
tions like this by taking the animal out of the wild but added it
might have been good if F&W or the landowner had built a den
of hay bales on the field and baited it, so that the bear would not
waste effort finding a den site.

3.

A member of the public
who lived outside
of the bear's belly
commented
that the farm girl in her
would have put the bear down.

4.

Then a wildlife biologist who had lived in the belly of many
different bears over a twenty-year period said, had you seen
this bear it would have been clear that he was an orphaned cub
starving and dehydrated. There is no way that he would have
been able to create a den. He did not have the weight or the coat
to aide him in hibernation:

wildlife experts
should have no question
about his age
eight months

wildlife experts who
aged him to be older or
assessed him
to be okay
only revealed that
they
did
not
have
the experience to be making
such statements.

5.

A gender conscience activist and member of the public from
inside the bear's belly commented that this bear had not been
in its natural habitat.

(S)he had been injured and
as a result her likelihood
of survival had been diminished

(s)he could not forage well
(due to its injuries)
(s)he was not
in her natural habitat
food sources being limited.

I don't think that the field between Hwy 1 and 22 is where (s)
he would have normally stayed if it weren't for her injuries.
There was so much stacked against this bear I felt it was our
responsibility to do our best to correct what we have wronged,
especially since there were facilities that exist to rehabilitate
him/her.

I have read
scientific studies that
support the full recovery and
reintroduction
of bears
into the wild

What studies and evidence did you base your reasoning on for
not rehabilitating the bear?

What evidence is there that supports a lasting effect of stress on
the bear that would have been detrimental to his/her survival?

I do feel that
the response
took too long.

So sad.

6.

I think the problem is that all sides in the debate are arguing
from a position of morality and ethics. Some have argued that

we had a moral duty to help the bear. I question the assumption
that we have a moral right to help the bear:

freedom is more important
to wild animals
than the fact that
some of us feel
compelled to help.

The decision to leave the bear unrescued was founded on
humility and respect for what it means to be wild, not on our
desire to feel better about ourselves:

everything dies, and in nature
many of those deaths are ugly
in my opinion
that's the bear's business
more than it is ours.

7.

We tend to think our domesticated lives are 'better' than 'wild'
lives, but really they're just what we've come to prefer:

wild doesn't just mean
as yet untamed
it is an entire way of being.

While, as an animal studies researcher that has lived inside
many bears, I appreciate feelings of compassion for other than
human animals and the desire to assist them, I think respecting
a wild animals' desire not to be in our sphere is paramount:

I don't know whether
bears suffer from
'capture myopathy'

though I don't know
why they wouldn't
but it is something
to keep in mind.

8.

I am not sure that we can say with certainty that the bear's
freedom is more important to it than our help or that humility
and respect and a desire to feel good about ourselves are not the
same thing?

Doing nothing made some feel better or at least wiser.

When predators in the wild come upon the injured they kill
and eat it.

When human animals come upon the injured we help or put it
down.

It is not in our nature to do nothing:

we gods rode in the bear's belly
debating our values and conventions
while the bear died a slow death
what was fair had no place.

9.

I feel now that I should have moved to the rear of the bears'
intestinal tract to be shat out onto the field so I could have
joined with the farm girl and either have helped or put the bear
down.

I CAME UPON A DEER

I came upon a deer
feeding on Thick-Headed Sedge
and Little Meadow-Foxtail

shut the truck down
watched for a while

it walked toward me
chewing
as deer do
looking
chewing
looking away
chewing
flicking its ears

it paused
I
positioned
my rifle
pulled the trigger

Spilling the hot guts
onto the cool forest floor
I unveiled the heart
and cut away the liver
set them gently
on a patch of dark green grass

I dragged the hollow carcass
to the roadside
lifted it into the bed of the truck
set the heart and liver
inside the cooling ribcage
then washed

the thickening blood
from my hands
in a shallow pond
of last night's rain

At home
I hung and skinned the deer
taking notice of the fat
along its spine

It will make good venison
once the meat has rested

I cleansed the carcass
of hair and blood
wrapped a cloth around it
to keep the flies away
thought about the hunted
we name prey

how they seldom die
of old age

thought about sedges and grass
and careful butcheries
and the real things we live by

I AM NOT A BUDDHIST

of any kind
only a fool
who studied
a few koans

and imagined
what attainment
would feel like
so I could keep warm

JOURNEY

The human heart is vast enough to contain all of the world. It
is valiant enough to bear the burden, but where is the courage
that would cast it off?
— Joseph Conrad, *Lord Jim*

When my journey is over
open the windows
to the winds that
took my life
air my clothes
on the line
so my coats flap and wave
frighten the birds away
so they will not shit on my clothes

Cry out to the mountains
to the heaving ocean
the rustling limbs of dancing firs
he is gone from here
he is gone from here

IN THE SHADE OF THE TRACTOR'S WHEEL

Each day my mother
delivered to the fields
where my father toiled
a midday meal
of hard-boiled eggs
coarse wheat bread
buttered yellow as barley
and slathered in wild raspberry jam

Coffee in mason jars
sweetened with molasses
thick with cow's cream
wrapped in newspaper
and towels
hot to touch

she popped the seal
from the jar
with the edge of the golden lid
poured it
let the fragrant liquid cool
before he sipped the edge
of the green glass cup

Strained muscles dust sin and sweat
washed away by that sweet drink
followed by a little sleep
in the shade of the tractor's wheel

NOT FOR THE DOG

*What heals ancestors is understanding them and under-
standing as well that it is not in heaven or in hell that the
ancestors are healed. They can only be healed inside of us.*
— Alice Walker

Father I hid from you
under a heavy blanket
your beatings still ringing in my head
swats from a bear of a man
who then dragged me by the ear
to the spruce tree grove
below the window
of my bedroom
where we knelt
and prayed to God
for a better understanding
of our place

I prayed that
my dog
would go to heaven

You put him down
upon the demand
of an enraged but
distant neighbour
for chasing cattle
though we all knew
it was not possible
"Boy" could have run them
and made it home
during the hour

we were gone
to church

I forgive you Father
because I know
how hard
it can be
to do the right thing

I forgive you Father
for your temper
for the clothes hanger bruises
the cuts made in love

I forgive you Father
for your trespasses

but not for the dog

ORDINARY

I grew up ordinary
the son of an immigrant
knew that things
were not that great
in the old country
for my father
the middle son of a harness maker
in a family of thirteen children
he left for America
found his way
to a small village in the Rockies

Worked the wheat farms on the plains
the road gangs when he could
homesteaded twenty acres
said to me
"I came to Canada
to be a Canadian, not a Dane,
don't want to sing those old songs."

guess he missed the whole point
of official multiculturalism
the Feds having decreed
that culture like baggage
comes from somewhere else

that didn't leave much room
for stories about place
cattle or road gangs

He said

"Multiculturalism's
just another way
to colonize the Indians
and wallow in
washed memories
of ugly places
left behind

might as well
give the land back to the Indians
for all immigrants
and their descendants
are at the least
guilty of crimes of the heart."

MY FATHER WHO ART IN HEAVEN

He had been weak for some time
cancer oh that demon cancer
working its way through his guts
then the terrifying phonecall
that said come to the hospital

It is time

My mother a nurse in Denmark
during the war
had seen death slip
into white rooms many times

us *boys* knew nothing of it

They let up on the morphine

and suddenly
he opened his greyblue eyes
realized we were there

asked us to hold his hands
while he led us in the "Lord's Prayer"
as he had done every morning
of our lives after devotions

"For thine is the kingdom
the power and the glory
for ever and ever, Amen."

He let out his breath
in a long sigh
that did not return

O death
still among us

we did not move
for a long time

TEMPORARY EFFECTS

Thought we
would live forever

but every once in a while
one of us dies

Because
it is his birthday

we hold a party
to celebrate

and no matter how drunk
we get or

lonely we dance or

loud we shout

no matter the temporary effects

the fact of his dying

remains clear
and unassailable

THE PARADOX OF DRONES

The evening news
shares the images of knowing

the kill has been successful

As in our children's games
the crosshairs found the target
ants running across
a desert of popping gunfire
those cars exploding
our enemies

We watch it again

and are given
to know those
who did the killing
are safe within
a paradox of drones
and distance

are given to understand
that our soldiers
are divine
but other than god

SOMETHING DIVINE

The Master and Monk are walking upon the mountain and
the Master asks, "Do you smell the mountain laurel?" "Yes."
"There, I have held nothing back from you."
— William Barrett, Zen for the West

The labyrinths of the intellect
quest for gadgets
techniques for externalizing life
the worship of blood
the hypermobility of postmodernisms'
revolution and doctrine
the spirit of paradox
not wanting yet knowing
the barbarism that screens
each night on public TV
is real

Lost in an electronic unity
of intellect and the senses
reason and intuition
morality and nature
God and creature
the Law and sin
the nagging conscience
dividing the rational mind from "the news"
watching carefully over the living facts
in the hop there is something divine
other than god
perhaps love

BLIND

You had just won the GG
me in awe

you told them
if they did not give it to you
you would kill yourself

I chose not to hear
what you had said

me the young poet
pleaded for my hero
to read my manuscript
instead threw it back at me
said it was shit

I chose not to hear
what you had said

Here we sit twenty years later
over bacon and eggs
a thin pane of glass
between us and the sidewalk
you telling me
you became an alcoholic
drank yourself into an ugly stupor
hiding forty pounders of vodka
in the garden
went through detox
finally grew up

"Ah jesus!," you said, "There was Al
on his death bed asking me
if I was his friend?"
Al had confessed
"I never had any friends."

"Al never let anybody be his friend
he could be such an asshole!"

So you have your memories
your garden
maybe some regrets
maybe not

heard a while ago
you were going blind
fuck man
you were always blind

COOKING

"What do you want for supper?"

I pulled back my chair
stretched a bit
looked into your eyes
past the question
to all I have
loved in you
and said
"You."

"That cannot be."
You said shaking your head
ever so slightly
from side to side

"Well then
how about a stew?"

Would that I
will always think of you
and you of me
when there is no cooking to do

OPPORTUNITIES FOR PLEASURE

Sometimes we make love
in a nest of brittle emotions
our hearts easily broken

sometimes we are
fully clothed
in anger and deceit

sometimes we are
naked as the breeze
and then there is nothing but

opportunities for pleasure

opportunities for pleasure

WINTER

It is an argument
about the size of the wood
we should burn
in the little black stove
that sits in the corner
of our living room

about the amount of heat
produced by a quick fire or
a slow burn

SWEET CUISINE

Caramelized deceit
dissolves slowly
in the hot pan
malodorous words
loiter in olive oil
mix with the smell of burning pots

Doors and windows open
we are clearing the air
enjoying salsa and
cool cilantro thoughts
the pungent yeast of rising bread
lips lingering tongue tasting
of sugar and buttered pastry
of lemon meringue

WHAT MATTERED MOST

After forty years of practice
our love making has become
slower more dignified

no longer
the passion of bodies
seeking unity

climax is a separate act
of declaration
quiets our restless bodies

This single act
is okay

Unity
as it turns out
is not physical
joint bank accounts
reciprocal wills and
division of labour
contribute more
to the commons

what mattered most
over time
was to know
we were loved

TRIANGULATION

After breakfast
after an hours' drive
after the first barbwire gate
has been closed behind us
we stand stretching our frames
in the darkness and watch
the flaring edge of the sun
touch the horizon
bring fire and frost
to the wind driven wheat grass
of world prairie

Looking west you say
the Diamond Willow hills
kneel before the Livingstone
that the Blackfoot
realized their location
by triangulating their position with
Big Chief and Crowsnest Mountain

then looking west toward the hills
you quietly avow
'I am looking for an idea
big enough to spend the effort
of writing another book.'

This is something I understand
now that age is feasting on us
for you a stainless steel knee
a new hip
for me an aortic stent-graft

manmade hoses to keep blood contained
and make living in paradise possible
How fortunate we are to face such dilemmas

Grim humour and hot coffee
chase the chill set free by the dew
we are survivors for the time being
lucky to be alive
we triangulate our location
mountains, prairie and the tailgate of the green truck

TREES

To live as a tree
is to live without fear
love or greed

if you have need of trees friend
take them
use them as you wish

build houses or beds or tables
burn them in your stoves to keep warm
ship them to others to do with as they will

make books to fill libraries with information
Trees are resting and nesting places for birds
beetles, animals, children, microorganisms

trees work well as metaphors and symbols for
what is imagined wild within worth saving
While hunting hot ideas to save ourselves

trees provide shade to cool the brain
so we can
consider the worth of forests

YVONNE'S MEADOW

I am not
an activist
am only one
of many small souls
who was acted upon

I saved no continents
waved no placards
did not go to jail for
my beliefs
did not demonstrate for *isms*
in front of cameras
wrestled into action
by videographers

I did not instruct
at colleges of higher learning
nor was I particularity good
at receiving instruction
I have no credentials
only a few incidents
I staked my life on

When I was young
I wore a uniform and
asked people to tie up their dogs
keep their campfires small

I walked in deserts
built trails in mountain country
climbed snowbound hills
wandered grasslands

botanized plants
stuck my nose into cities
collected my pay

I sang halleluiah with Cohen
while driving sweating trucks
down steep narrow roads
ran bright yellow machines
that moved the earth
packed and rode horses
into the wilderness

I wrote manuscripts
for bureaucrats and saviors
who overthrew me
learned to forget more than
they wanted to know

Yet one thing
I do remember
is the time
I watched you
standing in a mountain stream
gathering glacial water
into your hands
and pouring it over you
to wash away
the sweat of horse and fire

it was there I gave your name
to the meadow
high in the south fork
where we camped
and

watched the horses
jangle their way
to the stream
touch their muzzles to it
suck up water
and drink deeply

BONFIRE

We are gathered
at the cottage
by the lake
on a clear December night
to share a fire and dinner
with friends

George has built a beehive
of downed wood
gathered from the nearby forest
(as we age it seems
our bonfires grow larger)

We light up the night
and watch the flames
grow 'till millions
of glowing embers
rush the universe

Jenny says the Aborigines
ride the future
on such fiery constellations
that these meteor showers
can reveal our future

Our number
has grown smaller
as from our beds
we have worried
that the night
would not turn to morning
are thankful to be alive

We are survivors
gathered together

to remind each other
of whom we once were
gathered together
to burn the past year
each of us beautiful
each of us caring
for our memories
as we watch them
stream skyward
and light up the darkness